The Journey
Poems

Daniel Godward

Stackfreed
Press

I want to thank Jenny Kalahar. Without her help, patience, and belief, these books would not have come to fruition.

The Journey --- 1
The Spirit --- 2
Tell Me Why --- 3
The Envoy for Peace --- 5
Anna Nuvafing--- 6
Syria -- 7
War --- 8
The Displaced-- 9
The Somme-- 10
Armistice Day--- 11
Stay Alert --- 12
A Gift for Saint Nick-- 13
Crossroads -- 14
Life Unexpected -- 15
Anti All --- 16
Defined--- 17
Choices--- 18
Days -- 19
The Emperor's New Clothes -- 20
I'm a Blip--- 21
Assumptions and Presumptions -- 22
I'm Going Out -- 23
Hullaballoo or Kerfuffle-- 24
Friendship -- 25
Look at Life -- 26
Life --- 27
London Street --- 28
The Man from Across the Street -- 29
Magic Wand--- 31
Uncle Silas-- 32
Weeping Willow--- 34
No Superhero --- 36
Christmas --- 37
Cobblers -- 38
Now Here—Nowhere--- 39
Nowhere by the Sea--- 40
Right Honourables -- 41
323 --- 42
All Aboard the Gravy Train -- 43
MP Knocking --- 44
A Pious Fella-- 45

Black Lives Matter -- 46
Chicken Feed--- 47
Corona Nation --- 48
Donald's Cure-- 49
That's All We Have to Say --------------------------------------- 50
Lockdown -- 51
Fake News-- 52
Few Cases --- 53
Gone Too Far -- 54
Gravestones --- 55
I Am a Child --- 56
In This Together --- 57
Knees Up for Boris-- 58
Let Us Pray -- 59
Hear! Hear! -- 60
My Name Is ... -- 61
Peers of the Realm -- 62
Anthems --- 63
Staff Announcement ... Staff Announcement ------------------ 64
The Lights on the Dashboard are Turning Red --------------- 65
World Plague--- 66
Where Can the Children Play? ---------------------------------- 67
The Letter-- 68
Tortoise -- 69
Have a Nice Day--- 70
Old Versus the Young --- 71
Isolate --- 72
How Do You Do? --- 74
Universe Game -- 75
Hero --- 76
Metaphor-- 77
You Are Who You Are--- 78
My Favourite Child --- 79
I Raise a Glass -- 80
Lollygagging -- 81
Old Limehouse Days-- 82
The Virus is a Hoax -- 83
Mystery to Unravel-- 84
I Recall -- 85

The Journey

There's a lot to learn when life takes a turn
To a journey into the unknown.
You look back at what you had,
The good and the bad,
And it strips your priorities to the bone.
You see what really mattered,
That dreams can be shattered,
So your hands reach out for what's real.
In this strange life-and-death dance,
You pray for another chance
For the open wound to heal.
You look at the faces
Of those you love for traces
Of hope or despair in their eyes.
They're aware of your stare,
Of what you're looking for there,
For strength and love, and you realise
As a tear slides gently down your cheek
And wets an open lip as you go to speak
That there's no need for words, for there is nothing to say—
You just sip the love slowly, feel humble and lowly,
Grateful to see the dawning of
Another day.

The Spirit

His room is small, bare, and cold.
He sits by the window, in his chair, growing old.
The people, like the days of his life, pass him by.
So many, yet not any
Hear nor see him cry.

His flesh sags on his bones like a loosely fitted coat,
His skin folds and creases on his thin, protruding throat.
His scarce white hair and watery eyes appear
Ghostly through the pane,
Staring and despairing through the blackness and the rain.

His long-boned finger strokes a tear from his cheek,
Slides down to a trembling lip as though forbidding him to speak.
As a hammer hits an anvil, his arm falls to his side,
His eyes close, his breathing slows,
Another evening dies.

Tell Me Why

As you sit in your chair, are you aware
That there is a war going on over there?
Children are dying, mothers are crying,
Hope for mankind was replaced with despair.
As you watch your telly and fill your belly,
There is father holding his dead child in his arm.
He is screaming in anguish, you can see him languish,
To prevent his other children from coming to harm.
He's screaming, "This is my wife. She has just lost her life.
In the name of what did she have to die?"
Who sold these murderers the guns
To kill our daughters and sons?
Tell me why! Tell me why! Tell me why!
That was their nursery, that was their school;
We would watch them and wave at the gate.
Now they lie where they'd play,
In a bloody pool to justify somebody's hate.

As you sit in your chair watching his vacant stare,
Do you feel as numb as he?
Now his tears have dried, do you remember that he cried?
Do you feel numb or apathy?
What's going on over there? Do you really care?
After all, they speak a different language to you.
The church they worship in, different as their skin,
Who is their allegiance to?
The man holding his child just fell to his knees,
Screaming, "Stop selling the arms, help us, please."
If you feel you can't help, I beg of you try,
And if not, tell me why! Tell me why! Tell me why!
Hospitals, schools, homes destroyed.
Write articles on heroes when the troops are deployed,
Call the victims refugees of no fixed abode,
Watch them crawl down what's left of the road,
Holding fragments of what's left of the life they once led,
Holding together their families,
Their love, the wounds, that once bled.

As you sit in your chair holding your cup of tea in your hand,
I wonder if you can help me to understand
Why the politicians that we voted for
Profit at the loss of going to war.
Sometimes I think the end of hope for humanity is nigh.
Tell me why! Tell me why! Tell me why!
There is another child pulling at that father's coat,
Pointing a tiny finger at her brother's throat.
"Daddy, I don't seem to be able to make my brother open his eyes,
Talk to him daddy. Please, make him rise.
Please, Daddy wake him, don't let him die.
No! Daddy. No daddy. Why daddy? Why?"

The Envoy for Peace

The envoy for peace in the Middle East
Should get all to see the face of the beast,
To recognise evil, prevent destruction and fear,
Yet sees another chance to advance his career.
Who should we expect to promote war the least,
The envoy for peace in the Middle East?

Twice before he's taken his country to war,
Paddled in blood, yet still wants more.
Thousands of bodies lay dead at his feet.
Young fell like flies, to the war drumbeat.
He should wear a lamb's fleece, be flying white doves,
Yet the envoy for peace wears blood-soaked gloves.
Does he hear laments for the sacrificed, the names of the deceased?
Our envoy for peace in the Middle East.

Genocide of the masses, men full of revenge and hate.
Many killed by poison gases, he'd retaliate
With more bombs. Yes, the innocent will perish.
All that survives will be the oil to cherish.
He can drink his champagne and devour his feast—
Our envoy for peace in the Middle East.

When the bombs have fallen, who will leave alive?
Name one man who will survive.
Who will stand in the ashes of an annihilated race?
Blood dripping from his hand, a smile on his face.
Who will be left alive when the bombs have ceased?
Our envoy of peace in the Middle East.

Anna Nuvafing

I was in conversation with Anna Nuvafing,
As I ambled along the way.
When she finished talking,
I went to walk away,
"And another thing," she remarked,
For she still had more to say.
She talked of matter, and anti-matter in space,
Composition of the Milky Way.
Of extinct civilizations,
Of uncivilised nations,
How to keep colds at bay.
Of winged flightless creatures
With bird like features,
Of legends, myths and folklore.
Of the ant population,
Primeval soup of creation,
The hats at Ascot that ladies wore.
She talked of the numbers on trains,
The removal of stains,
Personality traits of each birth sign.
Of holiday slides, tramcar rides,
Of all the people that take shoe size nine.
Anna Nuvafing, Anna Nuvafing,
I'll hear that name for the rest of my life.
"And another thing," she'd say.
I can't get away!
Oh, Anna Nuvafing, she's my wife.

Syria

Have you heard the latest—what the newscaster just said?
In Syria, four hundred thousand are missing or dead.
One and a half million can now be labelled
As so severely injured that they are permanently disabled.
Those here in church, praying and singing hymns,
Pray for the eighty-six thousand who have lost their limbs.
All countries, politicians should be forever disgraced,
Seeing six million Syrians internally displaced.
So many innocents trapped and put to the sword.
Five million have managed to flee abroad.
Sunni Muslim majority have feelings that mirror and reflect
Those of the Shia Alawite sect.
Syrian government proud of their military capabilities.
Nearly five hundred attacks on medical facilities.
Syrian news agency says their people en masse,
Are pretending to be killed by nerve and chlorine gas.
Assad has solved his problem of high unemployment, unrest.
Save those on his side and kill the rest
Corruption and lack of political freedom,
Half a million dying or dead. jobs? They don't need them.
Have you heard the latest what the newscaster said?
One hundred and six thousand civilians are dead.
Atrocities in Syria have helped to nourish,
Jihadist groups al-quaeda, Islamic State to flourish.
Russia, Iran, Saudi Arabia, Turkey, U.S.
Have learned nothing from history to sort out this mess.
On countless bodies the victor will stand.
Have a panoramic view of a devastated land.
Those that survive will be alive but numb.
Is this how far humanity has come?

War

I read epitaphs of those the war killed.
Tried to imagine the ambitions and dreams of the young unfulfilled.
To think of what they might have been.
Tried to imagine the horror they would have seen.
To think of those who had survived.
The joys of youth they'd been deprived.
They cannot be seen, the invisible scars.
Their prison cells are see-through bars.
The generals behind the lines,
Placing teenage boys on fields of land-filled mines.
Moving men like chess pieces on a board,
Then say they died volunteering their lives of their own accord.
Strategic points valued in lives and limbs.
Their sacrifices sung in church with hymns.
Mothers sobbed from its pointlessness.
Fathers see minds and bodies destroyed by stress.
The thought of men in their twilight years,
Prepared to sacrifice youth to stem their fears.
To save their face, to maintain their pride,
To have their name recorded historically, glorified.
These politicians who retire at night,
Never hearing shells nor seeing the fight,
Not hearing an explosion or seeing a flash,
Flesh erosion, or a maggot-filled gash.
Each epitaph contained a rank and name
Of those who had been killed, but not of those to blame.
Those whose way of life was preserved while others cut short.
Respect should be reserved
For those who fought.
Not for politicians' statues carved in bronze.
But for those who were massacred at Ypres, left to rot at Mons,
Those who laid down their lives in every bloody war.
Time to remember what they died for.
Each country should now lay down arms; fighting should cease.
It's time politicians strived for world peace.

The Displaced

Fifty-one million people displaced,
Due to climate change, famine, and war.
The world watches and waits, aware of their fate,
Forming a disorderly queue at death's door.
They know there are lands where people are free,
From persecution, hunger, and thirst.
Thousands have lost their lives on land, at sea,
Praying this world is not cursed.
Millions being tarred with the same brush
As those they are attempting to flee
Because they have the same colour, language, religion,
They are holed like a pigeon;
Why not drown fifty-one million at sea?
We send money in aid which never arrives,
To plaster the scratch on the surface of human lives.
They sell the bullets and the guns
That kill their daughters and sons,
Calling them cockroaches so that our conscience can deflect.
The cause is nothing to do with us,
Say the monsters that cause the exodus,
And dehumanize those we fail to protect.
Send them back, send them home to the lands we invaded,
To lands we destabilised, and people degraded.
Send them back, send them home,
And turn our heads from their plight.
Make money from the war—that's not our fight.
We go in over there, come back to here.
We don't care; our conscience is clear.

The Somme

In the trenches they stood, shoulder to shoulder.
Their blood ran hot, their skin got colder.
Waiting for the signal, the shelling to stop.
The whistle to blow. The order to go over the top.
A cacophony of noise, yet they hear no sound.
Not the silent screams of men as shells explode all around.
Open mouths arid, too dry to swallow or spit.
Breath put on hold, lips being bit.
Men ready to run, scream, and yell.
Bayonets shaking as they brace themselves to run through hell.
Nineteen thousand, two hundred and forty would die this day.
Twenty thousand wounded the first hour, taken away.
This battle produced three hundred thousand dead.
One million casualties it's said.
They could have dropped one almighty bomb
To kill that many soldiers
At the battle of the Somme.

Armistice Day

The U.K. remembers Armistice Day.
Lay wreaths for the fallen in both world wars,
Yet count the pieces of gold,
Profit from bombs they've sold,
To warmongers on foreign shores.
For each bullet that's sold,
A body lies cold.
Thousands lie dead in a foreign field.
Innocents pay the cost. Generations lost.
Wounds inflicted that may never be healed.
Royalty leave their ivory towers
To lay their flowers,
In memory of children taken before their time.
The bullets and guns,
Kill foreigners' daughters and sons;
It's business as usual rather than crime.
Only ten countries in the world today not at war?
What do we have a Remembrance Day for?
Afghanistan, Iraq, Russia, Syria, Somalia, Ukraine.
The list goes on like carriages of a bloody train.
Turkey, Libya, United States, U.K.
Central African Republic, Congo, Cameroon.
All engaged in war today.
Colombia, Egypt, Pakistan.
Israel, Palestine, Iran.
We remember the dead one day a year,
And read what the epitaphs say.
We live but don't learn from what is said, I fear.
The world should wear a poppy every day.

Stay Alert

All week, I've stayed alert just like Boris said.
I've had no sleep, I could weep, and I've not been to bed.
I've secured the windows, locked the doors,
Blocked up the fireplace, sealed the floors.
I'm so tired! I just have to sleep,
But Boris said alert to keep!
For those tiny balls with little suckers,
To take no chances! They're crafty buggers.
Control the virus, don't let it control you?
What in the world am I supposed to do?
I'm not a scientist or magician—just a man.
But Boris has formed the shape of a plan.
I can wash my hands, but I can't touch my face,
Or see another member of the human race.
My eyes are red; my head's starting to hurt.
I've had enough of this bollocks—this staying alert!

A Gift for Saint Nick

Mum, there's a man in the High Street dressed as Santa Claus.
Doesn't he know about the lockdown laws?
He's keeping his distance but not wearing a mask,
And keeps taking sips from a metal flask.
He has holes in his shoes, and he's swearing, I think.
As he staggered by, he seemed to stink,
Of whiskey or gin—something alcoholic.
He was swaying a lot,
And seemed shambolic.
He's shouting, "Merry Christmas to all," and ringing a bell.
He fell down; he doesn't look very well.
I hear sirens, mum. Maybe the police were alerted.
Because of lockdown, the High Street's deserted.
He's thrown his beard onto the floor,
And slumped over outside the jeweller's door.
He looks wet and cold; he's making a sobbing sound.
As I passed him by, I gave him my pound.
He looked so sad, mum. He looked so sick.
Was it okay to give a present to Saint Nick?
He's placed it on his heart; he's giving me a smile.
That was all I had, but it makes it so worthwhile.
He murmured, "Thank you." He has a tear in his eye.
I didn't mean to make Santa cry.

Crossroads

He stood at the crossroads of heaven and hell,
Where he met a bookmaker's clerk.
He asked him which road he should take,
And was given this wry remark:
"One road is evil, one road is good,
The one you walked in life you must take,
If you've been neither bad nor good.
If you don't know which you should,
Then this decision you have to make.
It's even money which road you choose—
You can have two to one, no tax.
But once you decide which course to ride,
There can be no turning back."
"Well, for me, life on Earth was neither heaven nor hell,
For a gambler's life is in between.
I've seen men blessed, and I've seen men cursed,
While in the kingdom of limbo I've been."
Well, this is the final race for men,
For all who gamble with fate.
The going is heavy,
There's no betting levy,
The final course steward awaits.

Life Unexpected

Life is full of the unexpected,
Can often take a turn.
You may think you're always the guide,
But you're just along for the ride—
It's a lesson we all have to learn.
You may believe your fate is the design of man,
Or even life's eternal plan.
That you have an invisible benefactor, a reward giver,
Watching you float on a meandering river,
A tranquil river that swells with rain
To a turbulent river that subsides again.
You can stretch for the bank to rest and hide,
But like King Canute, you cannot control the tide.
The sea of life ebbs and flows,
You follow the route wherever it goes.
You can try to be observant,
foresee the current ahead,
See where the river winds, look for signs,
And hope the evening sky turns red.
The route your river takes,
Is shaped by success and mistakes—
Many that aren't your call.
Time is counted in fractions, passed with interactions,
Which can determine if you stand or fall.
We can only try to dictate our fate,
We all have a different river to navigate.
If there's one thing in life you need to learn,
It's that life can often take a turn.

Anti All

He's biased against
those taller than him,
But not just the highest, also those smaller than him.
Those fatter, those thinner.
A smiler, a laugher, more so a grinner.
Those whose hair is fair,
Black or white.
Mousy brown, dark or light.
Completely bald, or those who oil their head.
He can't stand those whose hair is red,
And who speak with a very posh voice.
Or a lisp, (yeth, he knows—they've got no choice.)
Those who end each sentence as if a question is asked.
Embezzling politicians who go about unmasked.
Men who take a drink, don't pay their way.
Those who talk a lot but have nothing say.
He's antiwar, anti-peace, anti-apathy—in fact, any cause he finds.
Basically, he's prejudiced against all of mankind.

Defined

I won't be defined by failure nor success,
What I have or what I've had, what I can't change or redress.
By cancer, by my age, by my height, by my weight,
By my accent, education, place of birth, or estate.
By where I live, what I drive, where I go for vacation,
By a sport, whom I support, by an acquaintance or relation.
But by who I am, what I am, in thought and feelings and in deeds,
Not taking life for granted, aware of what I've planted,
Knowing that actions and words are seeds.
What I love and respect and the values that I hold.
I can be defined by those, not fortunes of birth or a mould.
Ability to change, adapt, to learn as I grow;
Acquire strength, knowledge, aware of the seeds that I sow.
Eyes are a window to the soul, they say,
A window that should be clear and open every day.
Look inside, there's no place to hide—
See how straight the spiritual spine?
Then you'll know, this will show if one has walked a crooked line.
Our bodies are mere shells, armour for mind and our soul.
That is who we are, what we are, not our job or our role,
And at the end of your life you will be judged—
Defined, as you should.
All I pray, that those that know who know me say,
In essence, he was good.

Choices

What different lives we could have led
If we had made different choices.
If certain words had been said
Or we'd listened to different voices.
If we had made different choices,
What roads would we have tread?
The voices in our head—would we listen to what they say?
Would they take us far away to a place we were meant to be?
Would we listen to what they say if there was no mystery,
To a place we were meant to be—
How could we ever know?
If there were no mystery,
Would we even go?
How could we ever know
The road we should have took?
Would we really go
If life were an open book?

Days

I've had rainy days, sunny days, and some overcast.
Wet days, dry days, slow days, and some that go too fast.
Heavy days, light days. Dark days, bright days.
Confusing days, clear days,
Amusing days, tear days,
And some I think won't last.
I don't like to be consistent, nor insistent for routine.
I like life's variety, mixed society, an unexpected change of scene.
A selection of choices, faces, voices.
To watch life grow, to watch it change.
Watch it smile, even for just a while.
To embrace the new, welcome the strange.
But who would wish to know tomorrow,
To know in advance the pleasures and the sorrow?
I enjoy lazy days, sometimes crazy days,
Days which are not one thing or another.
If you were always aware of what is there,
Would you even bother?
Rain or sun, calm, or storm. Hope that none are the norm.
Peace and quiet, noise and strife,
Never be hateful, always be grateful,
For all the days of your life.

The Emperor's New Clothes

Everything today seems to be the emperor's new clothes.
People look at a thorn and think that it's a rose.
Pop singers who can't hold a tune,
Squeak like air released from a balloon.
Celebrities who get voted to govern,
Have photos in *Which* magazine with their coven.
Politicians who lie, cheat, and take us to war
Chafe not the wheat yet are re-elected once more.
Politicians draped in a golden fleece—
Sheep's clothing shaped for wear as an envoy for peace.
Football managers continually get sacked,
Actors, so-called, who just cannot act.
But they speak in a posh voice and are very well-connected.
Entertainers pay a penny in tax yet are very well-respected.
Boxers who can't box yet talk a good fight;
Their fans believe they might be right.
Ignorant people who pretend to have knowledge
Just because they attended a college.
People willing to tell you what to do for they say they know best,
They that represent you, but the money they invest—
Where they got it is not for the public to know;
That's not how they expect their interest to grow.
Judges of talent who themselves possess little
Break the dreams of the wannabes yet their own egos are brittle.
People need heroes and leaders to follow,
Hard on the outside, but inside are hollow.
Very few truly fit the bill.
So they eat what they're given—a bitter pill.
Look at the naked emperor and you cannot dispute,
That he's wearing his beautiful birthday suit.
Look at the storm; it's not good weather,
See the king, he is in the altogether.

I'm a Blip

If mankind is just a tiny blip in time,
Then all that the years that I live means that I'm
Just a tiny blip of a tiny blip,
Not even part of the flow—a minute drip.
That would mean that my wife is right.
A drip! So small that I'm out of sight.
She'll say she knew all along.
Bollocks! Is that woman ever wrong?
God, they say, hears us all and knows all what we do.
I've been married forty years, what else is new?
It's so hard to conceive. To understand
That I'm relatively smaller that a grain of sand.
Here for less than a twinkle, a blink of an eye.
What does that make me? What am I?
Do I have a purpose, do I have some meaning?
What was the point of birth and all that weaning?
Surely not just to grow, then to find a mate,
To get a mortgage, to procreate.
Well, I've done that and I'm still here,
Sitting at the bar, looking down at my beer.
I may not find the find the answer to the questions I'm posing
But I have a lot of time to ponder—the pub's far from closing.
Who am I? What am I? Why am I here?
As I sit on my stool yawning, the answer is dawning:
To watch the game and drink another beer.

Assumptions and Presumptions

I assume I presume too much, as such,
That I don't let facts get in the way.
I'm prone to believe
What I first conceive,
Oblivious to what others say.
If there's a light in the sky, it's a UFO.
I say it's a Yeti if I see footprints in the snow.
A handkerchief floating has to be a baby ghost.
I've seen Shakespeare's face in a slice of toast.
I know fairies have entranced me if I lose attention.
If I lose my keys, I believe they're in another dimension.
If I lay in and slumber so deep,
Obviously, aliens have abducted me in my sleep.
The fact remains that I'm out of touch,
But, I assume, they presume far too much.

I'm Going Out

I'm watching Dad putting salt on his bread and dripping,
Mum pouring hot tea into her saucer and sipping.
I'm spreading treacle on bread, for the crust we fought—
Best part of the loaf, my brother and I thought.
Neighbour's daughter's taking baby brother for a ride in the pram.
My sister sits on the step eating bread with white jam.
I run in to take the Brooke Bond card out of the tea.
Mum cut a mask from the cornflake packet for me.
An old iron man's shouting from his cart.
Dad's taking a nap, it gave him a start.
He's gone off again, I can hear him snore.
His tobacco roll-up went out, fell to the floor.
Mum's making pie with apple filling.
Electrics run out because we've not got a shilling.
Tar on the roads melting, it's hot today.
Got my ball. I'm going out to play.

Hullaballoo or Kerfuffle

You've asked me out for a pint. What do I do?
With the wife it could cause a hullaballoo.
Last thing I want is her feathers to ruffle.
And this might lead to a bit of a kerfuffle.
I don't want to cause an altercation or fuss,
Two weeks in a row might not be a plus.
I could just say I'm going out for one or two.
Surely that won't cause much of a to-do.
Three or four, she might not wear.
If any more, she would lose her hair.
I'll say I'm having one—word of honour, I swear, no more.
I don't think one will cause an uproar.
Last time it definitely did cause a slight commotion.
She, without doubt, displayed some negative emotion.
Yes, why not? I'll ask—no, I'll insist.
After all, last time I wasn't really all that pissed.
I was a bit light-hearted, happy, more carefree, I'd say.
It's not as if I get merry every day.
I'll make it clear, put it to her straight—
This decorating needs finishing, but it'll just have to wait.
Bye Luv, won't be long,
Popping up to the church for Evensong.

Friendship

To those who shared with me the gift of friendship,
Even for a while,
I hope the memories we made will never fade,
Will always make me smile.
Those unprepared moments we shared,
The laughter, the tears, the pleasure.
To those of you, old and new,
Thanks, they are my treasure.

Look at Life

You can look at life as a game,
No purpose, reason or aim.
You must use caution,
So you don't die of exhaustion,
Through playing too much of the same.
You can look at life as race,
All vying to gain a place.
If you set off too fast,
You'll chance finishing last.
Try to gauge your pace.
You can look at life as a simulation.
We're all programmed for reward, punishment, and stimulation.
But if we're not for real,
Who's turning the wheel?
Who's responsible for our creation?

Life

I know what life is all about.
It is those who have, and those without,
The rich who legislate, who set the law,
Set one for the rich, set two for the poor.
Set one, claim expenses, as much as the wage,
Lie, cheat and steal, and if at any stage
You get caught, raise your hands so they are not near the pocket,
If fined, find a way not to pay or to block it.
If you have incriminating expenses on your tax return,
For the next year they'll surely burn.
If you're worried about the care of your health,
Take out private insurance—you have the wealth.
So when you sell the health service, it's only fair,
Working-class sell their homes to pay for their care.
The young have no chance of buying a home of their own.
Those who commit this sin will soon atone,
Find themselves in debt, in let city,
Lost themselves in negative equity.
No chance then of inheritance, lest you count the wind.
Homes sold pay for healthcare for those who have sinned.
By being overweight or not keeping fit,
Their debts can inflate in their dingy bedsit.
Inheritance is paying for those they would not insure,
Who weren't in perfect health or who are too poor.
No health care, no home, the fate of the young.
From another hymn sheet this song is sung.
By the sermonising rich, the selfish devout.
I know what life is all about.
Encourage the young to have a university education.
Then hit them with the revelation
They will pay for the rest of the life they foresee.
The education tax, to get their degree.
They will wave it with pride and walk with backs bent.
Foot of the rich on their necks who will never relent.
From raising their snouts from the trough, except to pout.
Ah, yes—I know what life is all about.

London Street

I was a child in this East London street many years ago.
That's the corner where we'd all meet
To play Tin Can Tommy in the snow.
Birds were fed with stale old bread;
I remember the road as a carpet of sparrows.
Children fighting with swords made of wood, played Robin Hood
On pretend horses with bows and arrows.
Girls playing hopscotch, skipping to rhyme,
Boys playing ball against the wall.
It was three and in most of the time.
Dead legs, Chinese burns—I can still remember how that feels.
A cart made from an orange box, a plank, and old pram wheels.
We'd play marbles and lolly sticks, and everyone played E.
I was small and fast; it was hard to catch me.
This street was our universe, our world, our city, our town.
Sad to see it now, the old houses knocked down.
Cars seem to have replaced the children that played.
I was a child in this street where my memories were made.

The Man from Across the Street

Would you like to come over to my place?
I live just across the street.
I have friends and neighbours I would so like you to meet.
Walk this way—but not literally,
I do so because I'm stiff with cramp.
My muscles are rigid, my body so frigid,
Due to the cold and the damp.
That's why I cough and sneeze,
Splutter and wheeze.
The cold, it gets to my chest.
I take a sip of gin
To keep some warmth in,
Although hot food would serve me best.
Nearly there. See the arch? I'm the third cardboard box on the right.
We all share the brazier, though the flames get lazier
On the approach of the morning light.
Many roads lead to this place,
Many a journey to where we all abide.
This is the beach for us flotsam and jetsam,
Washed up on the human tide.
We are like krill in an ocean, aimlessly floating through stormy seas.
Yet remain in motion until we are washed up on our knees.
A myriad of stories of loss, pride, and pain,
Told in the cold, of the arches, over and over again.
Millions, I'll bet, who slip through the net,
Will end up in the gutter like me.

We sleep in the rain; we awake in pain.
We're the people that people don't see.
Loss of homes, jobs, and friends,
Too late for amends,
We take each day and night as they come.
Because we sleep rough people think we are tough,
But in reality, we are just numb.
Some look at us as if we deserve our lot
And so pity would just be a waste.
But we don't ask for pity in this cold-hearted city,

Just some understanding and less judgement in haste.
We realise, as people avert their eyes,
We're all regarded as unclean.
We know they look through us, they don't wish to view us,
So we remain unseen.
Here we are, it wasn't too far,
Share our food, our drink, and our heat.
I will introduce you as someone strange and new,
As the man from across the street.

Magic Wand

With a book of spells and a magic wand,
I took myself to the back of beyond.
I didn't expect to see much there,
But what I saw clenched my teeth and my hair.
There were charity and fast-food shops galore.
Estate agents, banks solicitors, and what's more,
Just to confirm my worst suspicions,
Every few yards a nail bar or opticians.
Bookmakers, pubs, parking meters.
Bakery shops full of pastry eaters.
Painted geriatrics with their hair bleached blonde.
Anyone want to buy a magic wand?

Uncle Silas

Last year, my uncle Silas died.
Dad smiled and cheered; poor Mum cried.
He said quietly, out of the side of his mouth,
Just when he thought things were heading south,
That we may be no longer be under the cosh.
That rich ol' miser should leave us some dosh.
Silas was a rich, tight old scrote
Who had a posh house and was worth a pound note.

We just had to wait for it to go to probate,
'Cause the ol' scrote named his parrot as next of kin.
We'd wish him well on his journey, get power of attorney,
He is Mum's brother, so we should be well in.

To his wealth I believed there was doubt,
But as it turns out, he weren't worth a bleedin' carrot.
On top, the cherry, he cost us money to bury,
But he left a jalopy and a hooligan parrot.

It screamed obscenities—some I'd not heard before,
And limericks too rude to mention or explain.
Silas didn't leave a will, and if looks could kill,
I think he would die all over again.

So we inherited the car, which by the way was tyre-less,
The obscene parrot, and a battered old wireless.
Like our deaf Nan, the reception was bad,
And like Nan, rattled and prattled and made Dad mad.
She said, "I can't stand this bloody wireless,
We should have buried it along with Uncle Silas."

Nan would scream "Eh!" each time the parrot swore.
It would repeat its curses, and then some more,
And with the radio blaring at full blast,
Call us all sorts of names twice as fast.

When I saw the mice move out in the night,
That was when I first suspected our plight.
Then Dad lost his job and signed on the dole.
The electric and gas cut off, and we had no coal.

Dad kicked the cat; the dog kicked the bucket.
Mum said, "Oh Dear!" The parrot said, "Damn it."
Nan's always giving Dad what for.
I really don't think I can take any more!

Then Nan slapping her gums as she makes an appearance,
Yelling about electrical interference.
I thought Dad would sigh less because of Uncle Silas,
Instead, wished Mum's relatives would bleedin' die less.

Then the solicitor called round, said he's found
Silas left a fortune in shares and stock,
And a big house, he said, and then the parrot dropped dead.
Dad's jaw dropped as well, in shock.

He said, "Stone the crows!" Gawd only knows
He does move in mysterious ways.
"Bless you Uncle Silas," and then he jumped on the wireless,
Got drunk and danced round the room in a daze.

To all my friends who might read this prose,
What the future holds, nobody knows.
Often laughter can follow a tear.
To my friends who read this,
Happy New Year!

Weeping Willow

My head on the pillow, the weeping willow,
Wept as I slept in my bed.
Dripping green spears, in a pool of tears,
The silence, the calm, lies dead.
The shadows that fell
Had a story to tell
Under the glow of a crescent moon.
Shrouded in lace,
Hanging in space,
Reflecting on the still lagoon.
A cur howls a lament,
As though giving vent,
To his loneliness on a barren hill.
The wood, silent and dark,
Awakes to a growl and a bark,
Then again, quiet and still.
Light touches my cheek,
My lips move to speak,
As I pull the sheet over my head.
In my purple sleep,
I inhale so deep,
Then sigh as morning and night are wed.
Curtains shiver,
The dog wakens to quiver
To the sound of the wings of a bat.
The rain left a stain,
Where it had run down the pane,
Watched curiously by the cat.
The star in the sky,
Winks with a curious eye,
Keeping vigil as I sleep.
Clear and bright in the night,
A lonely light,
Whose welcome company I keep.

My head on the pillow,
The weeping willow,
Who'd cried, now sighed,
In the morning rain.
My eyes open wide,
I rise from my hide,
To see the world through the windowpane.

No Superhero

I'm no superhero, son.
On a pedestal I don't belong.
I've tried to be good, as we all should,
To learn right from wrong.
There are things I regret,
Mistakes that I'd rather forget,
Times when I've been mistaken.
Battles lost and won,
Some that should not have begun,
And dreams that have been forsaken.
But, I suppose, I've made no more mistakes than most,
No more than others have I burnt the toast.
I did and do my best, that's all I can do,
I will always try to do that for you.
I just want to say, as father to child,
Life in its nature can sometimes be wild.
At times it's impossible to swim against the flow.
You struggle through the funnel,
Where the wind does blow.
There are rough waters,
But there can be tranquillity.
Calm before, after, a stormy sea.
Don't expect too much,
Just do your best.
You'll find the tide of life
Will do the rest.

Christmas

Christmas is a time for giving and forgiving.
Lending, spending, a high cost of living.
Rail strikes, energy hikes, Christmas songs played nonstop.
Not knowing what to buy, wanting to cry
As you slog from shop to shop.
Crackers are eaten, pulled, and told.
Good jokes, bad jokes,
New and old.
A time for make-believe and coloured lights,
Goblins and elves in red and green tights,
In curled up shoes and hats with bells,
Enchanted forests, wishing wells.
Not millionaire celebs on TV, radio, magazines,
With their ridiculously named children—spoilt brats in their teens,
Believing their opinions should be aired on the world's stage,
Listened to and tweeted by those on basic wage.
Not the well-known who moan and groan
Of their battles with drugs and drink.
They should be role models to youth,
Not vulgar, uncouth,
Bragging how low they can sink.
Not times to hear from the "Ins" and the "Outs,"
Or those on the fences,
Or politicians who warn of overspending,
As they submit inflated expenses.
The new addiction is social media,
Mobile phones, computer games,
Obsessions with crooks, cooks, fakers, and bakers,
Who become household names.
This is a time for friendships, no matter how far or near,
A time for giving and forgiving,
And appreciating those you hold most dear:
Your dart mates.

Cobblers

There was a cobbler on the cobbles
Who sold soled shoes.
He healed the well-heeled
To amuse as he mused.
He would lie as he lies
On the ground as he ground
His teeth together, wondering whether
The weather would be sound.
If sound, the sound he made
Could be heard by all hobblers.
This poem, when found, was found to be
Just a load of cobblers.

Now Here—Nowhere

I don't expect much, I'm not ambitious you see.
This is the place where teachers said I would be.
At last, I'm now here.
It's as expected, I fear,
But the journey … now that was another thing.
The adventure, the unknown, and life on the wing.
The risk of failure not spurring me on to win.
No anxiety, panic, nor thoughts in a spin,
I was focused and determined that I will get there.
I'm here.
I made it in life.
I got nowhere.

Nowhere by the Sea

I appear to be getting nowhere,
Somewhere I don't want to be.
But if I'm on the road to go there,
I wonder if it's by the sea.
I wonder who I'll know there,
I wonder who may know me.
I think of it, here and there.
And wonder where it could be.

What if it is nowhere to be found—
Will I be the one to find it?
I'll get nowhere, I'll be bound,
Or ahead of or behind it.
Perhaps I'm already there; this journey is in vain.
Maybe I'll get there, turn around,
Then go back again.
I'm sure it's not here on Earth,
At least nowhere I have been.
So if I find the way, I can truly say
It's nowhere to be seen.
I have no sorrow for tomorrow,
For nowhere is where I know I'll be.
But I don't care when I go there,
As long as it's by the sea.

Right Honourables

Sixty-four million benefit from the swelling of the NHS.
Seventy-one parliament members benefit from the selling of the NHS.
Promised directorships by those they truly represent,
And all they have to do is be a right honourable gent.
Sell it off in bits for profit and for personal gain,
To line their own pockets at the expense of people's pain.
Smile when cuts are made in services and staff,
All the way to the bank we can see them laugh.
The elected we trust to unselfishly lead
Cut and run, cut and run, and watch the people bleed.
Ambulances, care staff, nurses, see if your MP cares.
He'll be director of the company in which he owns the shares.
That makes the unkindest cut of all
That affects your family's life or health.
No conflict of interest, only interested in their wealth.
Sold the railway, sold the water, sold the reserve of gold,
Sold the electricity, sold the gas, leaving the elderly in the cold.
Five hundred nursing jobs so far, hear the MPs humming.
Watch them sing, watch them dance, the money train is coming.
No money in the pot they say, not a penny, not a cent.
£74,000 and expenses after their rise of eleven percent.
Will they be like care workers and get paid only when they work,
With no money for travel, expense accounts to unravel,
No second home as a perk?
Will they be like nurses, work a straight twelve-hour day,
Accept the same holidays and a freeze on pay?
The house recognises right honourable millionaires who come and go.
They will own the country—them and those in the know.
They play the party game; pass the parcel round to each other.
Parcel full of money. Hold this for four years, brother.
Which millionaire will you vote for,
Which one is honourable and true?
Which one wants to make the world a better place
And truly represents you.

323

If you were now or once an MP,
Would you want to be one of the 323
Who voted against giving nurses a rise,
Who now believe they can sanitize
Themselves of the disgraceful time when they all cheered
Along with Boris who stood and sneered?
I hope the words got stuck in their throats,
Saying nurses' pay was just a ruse to get votes.
Seventy percent of MPs have links with private health providers.
Do you trust they are honest law abiders?
All voted for health and social care act,
An action now too late to retract,
A bill to help privatise the NHS,
A bill they should now redress.
Now politicians hide in their toilets giving nurses a clap.
Stockpiling loo rolls because they talk such crap.
323—who actually can be named?
Cameron, Duncan Smith, Johnson,
And their cronies should all be ashamed.

All Aboard the Gravy Train

All aboard the gravy train! All aboard!
For all those made a Lord.
Take a leaflet for details of how to get away with fraud
With regard to expenses, room, and board.
All aboard the gravy train! All Aboard!
Wear a smug grin that you all can afford.
For those who have added gold to the Tory hoard,
This is your backhanded reward.
All aboard the gravy train! All aboard!
Book your holiday home, here, instead of abroad.
Honest men don't bother pulling the emergency cord,
Although most of them already have been put to the sword.
All aboard the gravy train! All Aboard!

MP Knocking

Mum, there's a politician knocking at the door.
He wants to know who you are going to vote for.
He's not from here, but he says he will fight tooth and claw
Because he empathizes with the working class
And represents the poor.
He's so well dressed and shiny, Mum. Him you can't ignore.
His class is middle England, Mum. He says he is the core.
He says where one is born is simply the luck of the draw,
but he said one would make himself heard if one gets to the floor.
He's prepared to keep talking until his throat is sore.
He has long-term plans, Mum, and will tell us exactly what's in store.
He's aware the MPs' expenses scandal is still a little raw,
But he will tell us how much our government makes
Selling arms to promote unrest and war.
He's promising the world, Mum. He's causing my hopes to soar,
He says the opposition is dull and dreary, just a crashing bore.
Mum, there's another politician coming, he says it is Sod's Law.
Is that a strange name for an MP? He says it really sticks in his craw,
that the other is indecisive, he's sure he's a neither and a nor.
He wants a relationship with the people nothing short of amour.
He won't constantly tell us what each party has done to keep a score.
He says the opposition are so funny, Mum,
They put the *f*s in guffaw.
What's that Mum? Shut the effin' door?
D-o-o-r, Mum. There's no *f* in—
Bang!

A Pious Fella

A pious fella left his cellar
To walk to church, but not for midday mass.
How did he look grasping the holy book,
Watching people choke by canisters of gas?
Peaceful protesters saying black lives matter
Were sent to scatter by thugs with riot shields and sticks.
There stands a thug with an air so smug,
Copying one of Hitler's tricks.
Christianity as a political tool is an old political game,
Encouraging violent response like an authoritarian ghoul,
All in Jesus's name.
Brutalise those who protest for a civil right,
But not those looting day and night.
Those who value their beliefs,
Who Stand for freedom from oppression,
Those from whom he would hide
Now cast aside
To lead his own procession.
His thugs attack as he pats himself on the back,
Waving a Bible in his hand.
He believes a murdered man would be his greatest fan,
Would say his economy is doing grand,
Has once again made America hate.
His advice? Don't be too nice, but violent against debate.
He sanctions police with tasers, guns and mace,
To brutalise those defending a race.
This is not a case of one bad apple,
But a police orchard rotten to the core.
Trees need uprooting and replanting to re-establish order
And uphold law.
He believes he has Christian soldiers
Marching on to war,
With the cross of Jesus
Kneeling to choke the Black and poor.

Black Lives Matter

I was there but didn't hear what was being said.
One moment he was alive, the next one, he was dead.
I didn't hear nor see violence, nor did I see him die.
I must have looked the other way,
Must have turned a blind eye.
I don't hear nor see racism if I look the other way.
I'm not racist myself, so what should I say?
I'm sure I didn't hear him gasping for breath.
I didn't witness violence, his murder, or his death,
Nor see the knee on his throat as he lay making no sound.
I was there, I admit, but I must have turned around.
You can't hold me responsible; I'm just a passer-by.
I neither hear, see, nor speak evil, and yet you ask me why
If I neither hear nor see then I'm not at fault.
You can't blame me! *I* did not assault.
For if I did hear and see and just stood idly by,
Watched him gasp for breath, watched him slowly die,
Then I would also be responsible and stand up for human rights.
I'd have to say Black lives matter, not just those of whites.

Chicken Feed

Prime Minister says his quarter of a million a year is chicken feed,
For writing a newspaper column is just poultry seed.
He gets this for a Sunday morning work and states this isn't too much,
Yet on women's pay and pension, he's not out of touch.
Women who have paid contributions for over thirty years, I've heard,
Who were born in the fifties have their pensions deferred.
MP's true salary and pension is over £100,000 a year.
Some retire on gold-plated pensions, I hear.
Former prime ministers can claim annually £115,000 in expenses.
Isn't it time the public woke up and came to their senses?
Assume a woman born in fifty-four became a nurse,
She paid in the national health over thirty years to the public purse.
Now she has to wait another six years and work a twelve-hour day
In order to survive, or lose her pay.
Women had this stolen with no notice given,
No chance to make arrangements or any other provision.
While Boris feeds his chickens on hundred pound notes,
He asks women in poverty if he can have their votes.
Women shouldn't complain, they say they sent a last-minute letter
Addressed, Dear Madam, or Ms future debtor,
Please ensure you don't get arthritis,
Ensure you can stand on your two feet
Or you'll end up in poverty, or out on the street.
MPs can't understand why women are making this ruck,
For under £10,000 a year, those fowl creatures don't give a cluck.
MPs earn an average of £27,000 a year, aside from parliament wages.
They could build a human zoo and feed women through cages.
They've all lost about £45,000 at least;
Let's see what the high court has to say.
As long as it doesn't affect MPs' expenses, pensions, perks, or pay.
I wonder when this went through. Where were women MPs?
I know it doesn't affect their wages or fees.
Oh! They were in parliament? Representing the poor?
That's what we have a democracy for.

Corona Nation

Time for celebration …
The queen's Corona nation's
In a right royal state
And it's too late to shut the gate.
Johnson's still allowing all to fly to where they like,
Or go by train, through a drain, or boat or bike or hike.
He doesn't want to affect tourism or Britain's purse,
So all are welcome with the dreaded lurgy—or even worse.
Come to Britain to have your fun,
No restrictions or testing need to be done.
He's left it to organisations to decide,
To stop the gamble or let it ride.
From China and Taiwan,
He's not learned lesson one.
He leads this farce,
With his head up his arse,
Which is why he's such a big rump,
Like his mentor, Donald Trump.
They both have a hunch that it's all a hoax,
And we can laugh at their epitaph:
"That's All Folks."

Donald's Cure

It will be fine if you inject a little pine,
Or Dettol directly into the vein.
And if that doesn't reach,
Try a little bleach
Straight into the lung. But then again,
What if you do? Then Trump might say
He didn't mean what he said yesterday.
He didn't say it would work—only said it might.
You'd burn and poison your insides,
But organs would be clean and white.
No, I'm sticking to taking malaria drugs,
Although they seem to be making me ill.
I'll stop those as soon as Donald suggests another pill.
The sun's gone in, and me too. No ultraviolet light.
I believe what Donald said, but I'm going to bed.
I really don't feel right.

That's All We Have to Say

A contribution to our party may see millions of pounds of contracts
When we put the NHS into the private sector.
If your donation is hearty, we'll give you the contacts,
When we put the NHS in the private sector
Each one of you could be a director.
When we retire as MPs, we're also directors of your companies,
So for now, no one can query our pay.
To wait, we can afford; it's all above board,
And that's all we have to say.
Private ops on the brain, the heart, and the liver,
We'll sell you the franchise, the public down the river.
Let's go forward on this, then it will be too late to reverse.
Pass the caviar, the champagne, and the public purse.
The righteous will frown as they watch many drown,
But that's the price one has to pay.
Houses in the country, and houses in town,
Time to write our expenses down,
That's all we have to say.
If we sell the NHS to companies that don't meet expectations,
They will have met them, in fact, for they've already bad reputations.
As long as they contribute via the back door,
We'll exempt them from tax; we can collect from the poor.
It's like paying for services in advance, in a roundabout way.
Let's not leave the public's health to chance.
That's all we have to say.

Lockdown

The old man didn't mind lockdown too much.
With his old friends, he was losing touch.
He'd send the odd message, made the odd call,
But it felt a bit like shouting down an empty hall
Where his voice may echo, rebound off locked doors,
Resound off walls, ceilings, and empty floors.
A wolf who had howled at the moon on a barren hill stood.
The lonely hoot of an owl in a far-away wood.
Going to call someone, in his usual way,
Then realised he had nothing new to say.
So he slowly stepped back from the hallway, closed the door,
Picked up a card that was lying on the floor.
He knew what the written words would say:
Try to keep the deadly virus at bay.
He knew there was no answer, no reply to send.
All he could do was pray for the pandemic to end.

Fake News

Donald Trump says hundreds of thousands will get better
By following these simple rules to the letter:
Go to work, or merely sit around,
There won't be a serious case to be found.
He knows just where this virus is heading,
And he says there's no chance of COVID-19 spreading.
In a few days, numbers reduced to zero.
Donald Trump, you are your country's hero.

Donald Trump has this virus under control.
There's not a person—not a living soul
Whose behaviour has to be restrained.
Donald Trump has this virus contained.
He can still hold a rally, still shake hands,
There'll be no victim tally,
On this, we know where he stands.
They're his followers, believers,
Of his wise words, receivers.
He makes them feel safe,
He makes their fear go.
Donald Trump, you are your country's hero.
Because he took action,
He was so prepared.
No sleepless nights,
No need to be scared.
This is not a pandemic; it's a political ruse,
It's certainly not systemic; it's merely fake news.
Rome is not burning, and he is not Nero.
Donald the fiddler, his country's hero.

Few Cases

Trump says there'd be far few cases, if any,
If there were no tests—or not very many.
Don't need swabs. Did his words get up your nose?
Open wide say "Ah," to swallow Donald's prose.
Who is that unmasked man who doesn't get the bug,
Protected by sunshine, disinfectant, and malaria drug?
Colorado alone saw thousands infected in a day.
He held a bally rally; he still had more to say.
To tell his mob he's done a really great job with the virus from China.
He believes George Floyd would say the economy today,
Like the police force, couldn't be finer.
That being said, he says stop counting the dead,
As one by one they fall.
There'll be very few cases, just thousands of faces,
Pasted on his wall.

Gone Too Far

This virus has gone too far, now.
My wife and I have no reason to row.
I can't go to the pub or have a bet,
Play snooker or darts, or ask her to let
Me watch boxing on telly or a footy game
Instead of a bloody bake-off, Ant and Dec.
You know who I blame?
The bleedin' Chinese. They could never play football,
Bloody table tennis, gymnastics, is where they put all
Their efforts, so they came up with
This virus to pull the rug
On all these sports—a super bug.
It could end all frictions, put an end to wars.
Bleedin' Chinese, they can still play table tennis indoors.
I can't even go out on a limb or a little bough.
This virus has gone too far, now.

Gravestones

The gravestones have tilted, flowers have wilted,
The names have eroded away.
The weeds are growing, there's no way of knowing
Who is lying here today.
Soldiers once sewn back together with stitches.
Bodies blown apart as they crouched in ditches.
Their blood mingled with rain formed a rose-coloured puddle.
Men screamed in pain as they died in a huddle.
Those men that then laid their lives down
From each road, each street, each village and town.
What would they think of us today,
Knowing their memories and names have faded away?
Underage children who naively volunteered,
Weren't mature enough to grow stubble of a moustache or beard.
They stood eager and proud to do their duty,
And saw the ugly face of humanity, the desecration of beauty.
They witnessed comrades and friends drained of their blood,
Limbs blown away in ditches of mud.
They witnessed Cane killing Abel, his brother.
Prayed after this war that there would be no other.
Every country but ten today are engaged in war;
They would wonder what they gave their lives for.
It was the war to end wars that we may live to say,
I wonder what they would think of us today.

I Am a Child

Why do you seem to hate the colour of my skin?
Why do you look without instead of within?
Does your religion not regard hatred as a sin?
Explain to me, for I am a child.

Do you hate the language that I speak?
Why do you worship the strong and despise the weak?
Why do you not see what is right and what is wrong?
Why chastise the meek?
Explain to me, for I am a child.

Why do you feel you can decide my fate?
Why do you carry a flame fuelled by hate?
Do you not want war and hatred to abate?
Explain; ease my pain … for I am a child.

In This Together

We're all in this together, David Cameron said.
In the same boat, all share the same bed,
Although while the working class are breaking their backs,
The upper classes … well, they pay no tax.
Not their fault, they're not to blame.
It's their accountants, they say, but just the same,
You'd think they'd suspect at a financial year's end
That there must be a reason they'd a touch more to spend.
Public transport fares may increase,
But doesn't effect these financially obese
Who travel by chauffeur-driven cars
To part-time jobs and subsidised bars.
They don't really care who is red or blue,
For it's one big party, unknown to you.
They're all friends and colleagues and went to the same school.
Can you believe the general public is such a fool?
The public sector gets a rise of one percent.
That would not do for a politician or city gent
Who get bonuses for failure and losing public money,
Then ask for more and think it's funny.
They say policies on liberty and privacy are sound,
And would sell your medical records for one pound.
Will politicians come clean about what they really earn?
Perks, expenses, and quangos give them money to burn.
They complain about their salaries yet retire millionaires,
Have gold-plated pensions that would help pay their fares—
That is, if they travelled by bus. Do they ever walk?
Although they're just like us, when you hear them talk,
They say when the country faces a storm and inclement weather,
Which is actually the norm, "We're in this together."

Knees Up for Boris

Boris Johnson says politicians
Should scourge themselves on their knees.
If they lie, like saying student nurses
Aren't paying extortionate fees.
Another untruth, hardly cursory,
That he restored student nurses' bursary.
He replaced it with a maintenance grant, yet,
Doesn't mention it puts student nurses' tens of thousands in debt.
Tories has invested billions in the NHS,
But compared to Labour, have invested less.
For any attending a hospital, he lies car parking is free.
That he increased child benefit. He did, by thirty-five P.
Fewer people now living in poverty, how many less poor?
None. In fact, increased to a million more.
He says no country has implemented track and trace.
A huge lie direct to the public face.
He should be down on his knees,
And not because his shoelaces need tying,
But because, once he again, he's bloody well lying.

Let Us Pray

Politicians that say they believe in God.
For their own backs, they make a rod
That holds them up, true and straight,
So they deal in love, and not in hate.
When they quote the scriptures and wave a Bible,
For what they say, they become libel.
When they say they act in the name of the God of love,
Let us pray He watches from above.
Let us pray they stop using their God's name to go to war.
They have guilt and shame for what they're killing for.
Pray we don't allow them to commit evil acts in the name of good.
Expose their deeds and the facts, so they behave as they should.
No matter what your religion, or even if you have none,
We won't be led by a hypocrite with a loaded gun.
Let us strip these politicians bare, but their shoes will be shod
So they can stand naked there, stand before their God.
We can watch them swear their actions are honest and true.
Every lie is bare before me and you.
They should act for mankind, for our and God's sake.
They would stand erect, true and straight,
Or find their backs bend and break.

Hear! Hear!

An MP can sit in the house yelling infantile abuse,
Guffaw and shout, "Hear! Hear!"
Stand and prance, take a childish stance,
Go to his subsidised bar for a beer.
MPs chat on the radio, perform on TV,
Write articles, attend functions, be a celebrity,
Yet have time to write down every penny they spend,
Keep all the receipts for literally everything they attend.
Serve on quangos, committees, company boards.
Represent cities where they don't live and have no accord.
I've come to a conclusion: I'm in confusion as to what they really do.
I know they talk a lot and balk a lot if as asked a question or two.
They take their noses out of the trough for the occasional cough,
And say they represent not themselves, but you.
These Hoorah Henrys, these chinless wonders,
Who we pay our money to,
What exactly do they earn, what really is their game?
They say the working class have a voice,
The working class have a choice,
That they aren't all the same.
They rehearse their lies the speech writer composes,
Practise deflection and misdirection.
They lick the gilt and guilt off each other's noses,
Lift their alter egos for inspection.
To us they're on an entirely different plain—
A cattle truck to a first-class train.
"Hoorah! Here, here," words they repeat over and over again.
Does anyone care for a glass of champagne?

My Name Is ...
(In the voice of Michael Caine)

My name is Boris Johnson, I mostly work from home.
That's why I never brush my hair or even use a comb.
What I'd like all of you to do, is to be alert.
You can go to work if you're a doctor or nurse
Or if you wear a white or blue collar shirt.
The rest of you stay indoors
Unless, of course, you're going out
To buy essentials, or incidentals,
'Cause there's a silent mugger about.
So until the herds immune you can't commune,
You can be in the all together.
All I ask is that you wear a mask,
Which you can buy on the Never Never.
Save the NHS—they saved me
A few bob not getting treated by private health.
I applaud 'em, I will reward 'em,
By later selling it 'orf by stealth.
Lastly, regarding work, rest, and play,
You can exercise twice a day.
Remember—be on the lookout,
Be alert, wherever you may roam.
My name is Boris Johnson, and
I mostly work from home.

Peers of the Realm

My lords with maladies, not gentlemen,
I cannot call you all by name.
Just as the expensive sleaze of our British MPs,
It appears you peers also have no shame.
You believe the public are mad, stupid, or lost their senses
When you cross the road to claim your expenses.
You walk from mortgage-free homes, yet say you live in the county,
Signing in for ten minutes to claim your bounty.
If you do stay longer, what is it that you do
Besides business deals that just benefit you?
Do you go to prostitutes for your jollies or drugs?
You believe the public are apathetic or downright mugs.
So many of you are caught committing a fraud,
Yet you all still have no shame, and call yourselves lord.
None of you can comment, you're all away on vacation,
Yet still have the gall to comment on the state of the nation.
House of Commons, House of Lords,
You're both just the bloody same.
Neither of your houses have any shame.

Anthems

Anthems sung by the old and the young,
In different countries, in a different tongue.
Hope for the future in the country where they abide.
Made possible by the old and the young who have died.
Those young who died that the old would be proud.
Many millions were wrapped in their national shroud,
And many millions were laid saluting their flag—
Laid at attention in their body bag.
For if others sang a different song,
For a different land where they belong,
If they had different religion, language, colour of skin,
Different clothing, tradition, or hair on their chin,
Then they are alien, foreign, not the same,
If they have a different view, then they are to blame.
The old who find it easy to hate the lot,
Under the guise of being a patriot,
Don't question their leaders, who can't be wrong,
Would annihilate those who sing a different song.
Who salute a banner, a pennant, cloth, or a rag,
That's different to their ensign, their national flag?
If their leaders say it's now the killing season,
If you question their motives, it will be regarded as treason.
It's unpatriotic, disloyal, morally wrong
To dispute the motive of war against those who sing a different song.
So go to war or risk being named and shamed.
If we lose, then it is you who will be blamed.
Go kill the foreigner's daughters, the alien's sons,
The grandchildren, nephews and nieces—fire the guns
At their sisters, their brothers, the fathers the mothers,
Honour and obey your warmongering leaders.
Only hear what they say, the young blood feeders,
For they are all knowing, all seeing.
Be the flag, be the song, not a human being.
I hope one day all countries will sing the same song,
Wave the same flag, that they all belong
To the land they share on this globe in space,
For if man can't share, then it's the end
Of the human race.

Staff Announcement ... Staff Announcement

"Would Tony Blair please go to aisle I for Iraq?
There's a major blood spillage, he is required to attack.
Take pen and paper to make a list."
M'lord could also go to assist,
As he believes every word that Blair has said.
Could he help mop up the million or so dead?
He may find wee aprons of mass distraction,
Stained in blood as they've been in action.
But he can clean up by talking about his job,
Close the door so we don't hear relatives sob.
Dead silence please, while Blair's on his knees.
Don't bother, he's only checking his consultancy fees.
He'll need a scrubbing brush to get his hands clean.
"Blair needed in aisle I for Iraq." But he cannot be seen.
He's be engaged in a business deal if he cannot be found.
"Blair to aisle I for Iraq. Blood is soaking into the ground."
He may be hiding behind a bush, or even found in denial,
Or practising a defense speech for any upcoming trial.
He'll need the right equipment—old stock won't suffice.
He could first send an inspector, listen to advice.
"Tony Blair, go now to aisle I for Iraq,
Then proceed to the Afghanistan aisle.
Bodies need a pull and a push; someone could make a pile.
Blair, go to aisle I for Iraq. Find it in the Middle East somewhere."
A statue torn to the ground, a statue of Tony Blair.
It's best he does what he thinks is right at this time.
If he believes it's right, it can't be a crime.
Was bending to Bush putting lives at risk?
What else was he risking, just a slipped disc?
Every day there are more bodies, the injured keep coming back.
"Tony Blair to aisle I for Iraq."

The Lights on the Dashboard are Turning Red

The lights on the dashboard are turning red.
May be a world recession, David Cameron said.
Europe is weak, we must prepare our defence,
So we'll give away two billion. That makes sense.
We can't cut taxes for middle or working class.
They must play their part in this political farce.
Treading carefully, for we cannot afford
Exemption, except for the companies who set up branches abroad.
Let them claim expenses for the funding of those,
With a loss of British jobs. Yes, I suppose.
To countries with a lower corporate tax rate,
Axe the tax they pay here; that should negate
The debt we owe for funding our election campaign.
The other parties know, but they don't complain.
Government set up seven committees to oversee corporate tax.
Execs of banks and top companies must scratch their backs.
For the financial support given to the party, we pay them back *tenfold*,
Their job is supposed to be public service—
Servants who do as their told
By those, the country's financial elite,
Who can give politicians directorships. And when they get beat?
May be hard times ahead, we must prepare,
Stand fast, said the chinless multimillionaire.
Farage, Cameron, Miliband all make me nervous,
For they all want to destroy our National Health Service.
Not a straight answer to any question. They all have a forked tongue.
Would they slice the throats of the aged, dash the hopes of the young?
They are entwined with us as servants or masters, a convolution,
When the wheel turns, it's called revolution.
They will sell our public forests and records of health
To absorb more power, to gain more wealth.
They may just stop at selling your heart and your liver,
But not at selling Britain down the river.
The lights on the dashboard are turning red,
But their bank balances are black as an oil bed.

World Plague

Do you remember the world plague,
When the prime minister was vague
About the future of the NHS?
Most MPs would benefit from its demise.
They voted against giving staff a rise.
For the nation's health, they couldn't care less.
They cared about profit. They stood to share,
From investments they made in private care.
Hoped to clean up doing deals with the USA.
Staff moral low, they're on their knees to pray.
Corona virus started spreading.
They knew where from,
Where it was heading.
Knew NHS staff had no protection or machines.
Staff had the will but had not the means.
Flights allowed to come and go,
Clueless how to stop the virus or make it slow.
Collateral damage, a sacrifice to make.
Losing staff and patience … a chance to take.
The stock market had to be kept afloat
As they played the game of chance on the luxury boat.
Doctors, nurses would stand and fall—
A poker game to raise and call.
Now MPs watch the fear and panic
As if watching the sinking of the Titanic.
Peep out of the window of their private ward,
Make a feeble attempt to smile and applaud.
They shout, "Bravo! Well done! Good show!"
To NHS staff as bodies flow.
When the nightmares are over will they just regress
And use the plague as an excuse to sell the NHS?
Or will they protect what we hold most dear—
For once be honest and sincere?
Or will they put money aside to bail out banks?
Or be humble? Grateful?
Maybe give thanks?

Where Can the Children Play?

I live in a room ten stories high.
The ground seems further away than the sky.
You can see for miles and miles away,
But where can the children play?

The corridors are long, the balconies are wide.
When they play hide and seek,
There's nowhere to hide.
They make too much noise, so the neighbours say,
But where can the children play?

There's a park down below made of stone.
Cold concrete where grass had once grown.
As the sky leaves no trace of where a bird has flown,
Where have all the children played?

The Letter

I am writing this letter to explain
The purpose of writing this letter.
For the most part,
The substance contained
Is to give you insight
For the reason I write.
To that end, it could not be better,
Or more explicit, clear, and concise.
It could not be more lucid and plain.
I could not write you this note if
I had no real motive,
So I wrote this note
To explain.

Tortoise

I remember the teacher that taught us;
Too slow to catch or report us.
He carried a large shell, but he taught us well,
And was always there to support us.
A good teacher, he, that tortoise.
On our side, and never fought us.
He was so patient and wise,
With all-knowing eyes,
Knowledge was all he brought us.
We were pupils for he, that tortoise.
He was faithful, would not abort us.
He was loyal and true,
Shared the knowledge he knew,
And not fault us baby tortoises.

Have a Nice Day

You're telling me to have a nice day?
My daughter with a drug-dealing pimp's run away!
I've just lost my job, they're cutting down on staff,
I thought it was joke, they were having a laugh.
They said they were making cuts? Well, they can't go any deeper.
I'm a ruddy lighthouse keeper.
So now I have no job. I could go on the dole then,
But can't drive to sign on, my bloody car's been stolen.
It's not insured, it is a Rolls Royce,
On top of that, my wife's a singer and she's lost her voice.
In debt up to my eyes, under the cosh.
I owe the bookies a pile of dosh.
My son smokes pot, works in a theatre foyer.
Won't let anyone in, he has paranoia.
I own racehorses, but they all have cholic.
Got a full wine cellar, I'm an alcoholic.
Doctor just put me under sedation,
Because my father died recently of leprosy and dehydration.
He also passed on a genetic disorder.
He left me out of his will. He was a compulsive hoarder
Of valuable art and precious stones.
My best racehorse has been diagnosed with brittle bones.
My wife is so frightening she has to be defanged.
My psychopathic brother is due to be hanged.
There was an earthquake last week, my house was destroyed,
And all that's left is an empty void.
You? You're just an answering machine for ruddy banks.
If I leave you this message, you'll give me your thanks
In your patronising voice, condescending tone.
Why not put a human being on the ruddy phone?
Now that I've said all I have to say,
I really do think I might have a nice day.

Old Versus the Young

The young care if they're broad, tall, thin, or small,
And even if a hair is out of place.
The old only care
If they still have hair—
Usually here and there on their face.
Young sport a five-o'clock shadow.
(I'm referring to the males.)
The old use razors, blazers, and braces,
Usually bought in the sales.
Young pay exorbitant prices for a pair of bumpers,
Even more to have a certain motif on jumpers.
Tee shirts with strangers' names printed front and back.
Old happy to wear an ancient Mac.
Some wear designer gear to show what they can afford,
And roam Carnaby Street wearing this sandwich board.
The old wear just about the same as their peers,
Any old clobber they've had for years.
Maybe an item or two of fashionable "smutter"
Which stands out alarmingly in a wardrobe of clutter.
Young listen to a screaming band.
Old, a melody with words they can understand.
Young eat Turkish and Thai food exotic.
Old eat turkey, pies, and a probiotic.
Paying treble price for a shot in a wine bar, the young think is class.
The old? Just stout—real ale in a glass.
Young wear skimpy clothes in the cold that show their form.
The old wear wool to keep them warm.
Young spend fortunes on multiple tattoos
While the old buy cider vinegar, comfortable shoes.
Young listen to same songs repeated each day.
Old, a comedy, the news, or a play.
They both look at each other as if each are strange,
Wondering how taste can so drastically change.
Thankfully they do, or you'll have sheep in lamb's clothing.
Even worse, lambs in sheep's—more loathing!
So if you're young, but growing old,
Don't let it get you down.
Don't become the oldest swinger in your town.

Isolate

My wife asked, "Why so late?"
I said, "Please don't make a fuss. I missed the bus,
Then I had to wait."
I couldn't use the public phone to phone her—
I didn't want to fall prone to the corona.
That's the reason why I'm so late.
"My mobile had run out of charge again,
Then it started to pour with rain.
I stood at the bus stop and got soaked through.
I didn't want to be late for you.
As we couldn't talk,
I decided to walk.
Squelched along the road.
Now here's the rub,
I was the passing the pub,
Publican was struggling to lift a heavy load.
My innkeeper friend just had a delivery of beer.
He asked, 'Can you help carry some crates in here?'
I agreed, for I'm sure you understand,
I still had a little time on hand.
Although the pubs had been closed thus far,
Would I help him to restock the bar?
I did, so in gratitude he poured me a pint of beer.
I steadfastly refused it, proclaiming 'This is not the time, I fear.'
He's a mate, so what was I supposed to do?
But I still refused, fearing I'd be late for you.
Well, as he had poured it already,
And it looked so lively and quite heady,
I really didn't want it to go flat.
I allowed two sips to pass my lips,
Then I put on my thinking hat.
I decided it was too impolite to refuse;
I never before turned down free booze.
I didn't want to set a precedent,
And just one pint won't hurt in a one-off event.
I had ale, he had lager and lime.
I downed mine in one with one eye on the time.

He poured another before I could say no.
My eye left my watch—can't believe how fast time can go!
He said there was no need to trudge to the bus stop again,
Go out, get soaked into the pouring rain.
It was after maybe three or four more,
I was able to stagger to the door.
Although he said he'd drive me to our tryst,
He yelled 'I can't bleedin' drive! I'm too bloody pissed.'
Now realising I wouldn't arrive on time,
Quite rightly, you'd see that as a sin or a crime.
I felt afraid, so for Dutch courage I sank one more.
I bade adieu, staggered out the door.
That certainly appeared to do the trick.
I was feeling brave, but slightly sick.
I hailed a cab, said, 'Save me from a berating.
Take me to my one love who I know is waiting.'
So here I am, slightly overdue, my love.
Mask upside down, a bit askew, my love.
Call it kismet, preordained, call it fate,
Givush a kish.
Shorry I'm late."

How Do You Do?

"How do you do? How are things with you?"
Asked the toad of the kangaroo.
"Oh! Up and down, you know. It's the only way to go.
How are things with you?"
"If I'm down, I always bounce back,
I try very hard to keep on track.
I can take a leap of faith, a leap in the dark.
If you believe in the universe, life's a walk in the park.
Although you don't actually walk; neither do I.
Stand on one limb? I wouldn't try.
I agree, you see, that we are bound,
To keep both feet on the ground.
To be strong and firm—do not flounder.
You're a friend, but you're indeed a bounder."
"A very nice chap," toad was heard to say.
"Goodbye kangaroo." Then he bounded away.

Universe Game

You may believe you're in control of your life each day,
Except for the odd moment or two.
Open your eyes, you'll realise,
There are forces that are guiding you.
In those, have faith, trust, and believe,
There are never two days the same.
Life is a river that flows,
Watch where it goes,
To play the universe game.
The universe smiles on those who see its game each day.
Who enjoy each moment and watch the play.
They are always surprised and cannot comprehend,
How each day's story unfolds and reaches its end.
Not by design, guiding, or aim,
But simply by playing the universe game.

Hero

He now has a title, has now been renamed.
That is, since he'd been injured, since he'd been maimed
In that unarmoured jeep, blown up by a bomb.
Now not called by a number or his name, Tom.
Now he's a statistic, he now has a label.
A name to write on a card at the dinner table.
But the politicians would not send their sons
To fight with inadequate equipment, facing enemy guns.
They say it is treason or disloyal to criticise,
To say the truth and expose their lies.
They claim expenses for their sons, daughters, and wives,
Money that could have been well spent saving young lives.
MPs claim for wallpaper, newspaper, toilet paper, and booze,
Yet troops go to war wearing inadequate shoes.
MPs do their stint in the house between radio and TV,
Wining and dining as directors of a company.
They are paid for committees
And quangos of which we aren't entitled to know,
Of what is said or done, how much they are paid to go.
We know what Tom was paid to go to Afghanistan,
What he can claim as a crippled man.
He lost his legs; he lost some friends.
Money's not enough to make amends.
Tom knows first-hand that the cost of war is steep,
Yet young lives, like politicians' words, are cheap.
They give him a new name now, a name that ends with a zero.
Smile and say
As they walk away,
"That man is a hero."

Metaphor

I'm trying to think of a metaphor,
Of the point where further is no more.
When you're as far as you can go, standing on the edge,
Peering far below, teetering on the ledge.
The place where you stand or fall,
And lean with your back against the wall.
On the cusp, at the rim,
No choice but to go with the flow—sink or swim.
No skill or knowledge will help; there's nothing to learn.
You're at the point of no return.
How many of us are tested and can say whether
They will or won't snap at the end of their tether?
Stare deep into the void, try to see through the dark and the mist.
Take a leap of faith, pray someone will grab your wrist.
I'd think of my children, think of my wife.
If death comes, I'd say … that's life.

You Are Who You Are

You are who you are, unique and strange.
You've been shaped, but your shape's always open to change.
At the end of each day, you may reflect on what you've lost and won.
These should be laid aside before the next day's begun.
Both are illusions, dreams in your mind.
To go head unencumbered, you must leave both behind.
Choose wisely the words you say
You may think they float away in the air,
But to those you say them to, they will always be there.
On what you do, you may also reflect,
With whom and to whom you do them will have an effect.
Be positive and humble for all that comes your way.
Appreciate your life, as if you only had that day.
That one day alone, with no time for negative thoughts,
For people are like days—a multitude, of sorts.
Take each night, day, and person as they come.
The sighted, the blind, the deaf and the dumb.
What they speak of may be peculiar to you,
But try to listen and learn; see a different view.
Treasure each moment, be they high and low.
Don't carry them on your back wherever you may go.
Give yourself permission to feel and see good.
To know you've shared this feeling as much as you could.
Know what is precious, like health, love, knowledge, and time.
To watch it flow and to know you're a small part of this rhyme.
Learn to say you love this life without making make a sound.
This journey, this circle, this one go 'round.

My Favourite Child

You are my favourite child,
Most intelligent of all.
Whatever I do, whatever I wear,
You always think I'm cool.
You never say I'm embarrassing,
You think I'm intelligent and quite a chap.
You're not like the other two
Who say I'm always talking crap.
You admit I'm the best at games and sport,
You show me deference, utmost respect.
When I ramble and I shamble, you never seem to object.
You think it's always nice when I give advice,
And hang onto my every word.
You know it's fact and wouldn't retract
That I've ever said a thing absurd.
I pick the very best films on channels for men.
For my music taste, you would always give me a ten.
You envy my style in clothes, my understanding of world affairs.
You believe dads like me are so unique, you wish we came in pairs.
Even when tipsy, I conduct myself well,
And have always been a right chap.
But most of all, you're my favourite child
'Cause you say I never, never talk crap.

I Raise a Glass

Those friends out there, honest and true,
Who have allowed me to share some time with you.
I hope your hand of friendship will never crumble.
As we grow, I grow ever more humble.
For I realise as time itself makes me old,
Real treasures are not of silver and gold.
Not tangible, visible, possible to touch.
The real wealth, like health, is what means so much.
Not an object to flaunt, to show or wear,
But an unseen force you know is there.
If this feeling is in your heart and mind,
It's the greatest gift you can ever find.
For all of you, those who shine in the darkest night,
I raise my glass of wine to your glowing light.
I feel grateful and blessed for each year's end.
For each week, each day, each moment, each friend.

Lollygagging

My girl accused me of lollygagging,
As if taking it slow were a crime.
She said I am prone to procrastinate,
That I'm always late,
That I have no sense of time.
It's true; I hardly ever get anywhere in advance.
If I ever did, then it would only be by chance.
I know I'm kind of prone to postpone.
I tend to put off till tomorrow.
I say, "Why not delay what you do today?"
Then look forward to what may follow.
When I turn up, she does look
As if she has a tail that's wagging.
You know what? Secretly, I think
She likes me lollygagging.

Old Limehouse Days

In days gone by, I remember the whistling kettle,
And when soldiers and model cars were made of metal.
We roasted potatoes on the fire, sat by the hearth,
Each week went to a swimming centre to have a bath.
A penny bought a slice of toast and a cup of Oxo gravy.
Mum curled my hair with hot tongs to make it wavy.
Carrier bags were made of paper.
If electricity strikes, we lit candles with taper.
Coal strikes, we dug up tarry blocks from the old bombed park.
Played as late as we could in the street until dark.
Listened to the radio before going to bed;
Comedy or music. Sometimes I read
Enid Blyton books, Sherlock Holmes.
I remember chiming clocks
Big plastic combs.
I loved reading Lewis Carroll and Edward Lear.
Nonsense poems still ring in my ear.
I loved made-up words of people and places.
They described them so well, I could see their faces.
Days of the past weren't always good.
But if I could relive some of those times, I certainly would.

The Virus is a Hoax

Donald Trump said the virus is a hoax.
So I thought I'd wander down the pub,
Have a beer, tell some jokes.
I left my house full of hope and smiles,
Set off to walk uphill five miles.
I did wear gloves, scarf around my face.
Had a two-metre stick, just in case.
You won't believe it—the doors were shut!
No one there sober, never mind half-cut.
Then it started to rain, and I mean torrential.
Police stopped me and asked if my journey's essential.
I said yes! I want beer. Trump said the pandemic is over.
I can't believe they threw me in the back of a Rover.
They asked me where I live, I said, "I go straight and fork off."
They said, "Go and do that then, don't sneeze or cough."
I got home soaked through. I did have the hump
All because I believed Donald bloody Trump.

Mystery to Unravel

We do not choose on which street we are born,
But we can choose the road on which we travel.
Paths of stone or sand, which turn to take
Is a mystery to unravel.
There's no way clear to see what lies ahead,
The highs and lows, around the bends,
If we should lead or indeed be led,
Nor where the journey ends.
We can learn as we go, use what we know,
To try to navigate our way through.
Sometimes seeds are sewn to grow the unknown,
When attempting something new.
As you mature with age, having reached each stage,
Priorities may change.
Each hill you climb
Becomes a unique time
Where the familiar can appear strange.
What you see and how we see it,
Often depends from where we view.
What we want to become and how we become it
Mostly depends on you.

I Recall

I look back at my youth, and I recall
What life was like when I was small.
Little legs spinning on my three-wheeled bike,
Wearing the Davy Crockett hat I used to like.
The feel of lead soldiers and cast iron toys,
Playing cowboys and Indians with the other boys.
Grown-ups were as big as giants, all had a certain smell.
Who they were with my eyes closed, I could tell.
The four-year-old girl who lived upstairs
Played with dolls and teddy bears.
She was my very best friend,
And when I learned to write, love notes I'd send.
I'd dream of one day owning roller skates,
To roll along the street with my mates.
Girls sang songs while skipping.
Mum put salt on bread and dripping.
I had white jam or treacle on my bread.
The crust always had to go to my brother, he said.
Not of course if I bagged it first,
Then he would pinch my arm.
I think a Chinese burn was the worst.
We would race up the street; I never won.
I'd pretend to shoot him with my toy gun.
He made a cart and we took turns to ride.
He won a goldfish once
that quickly died.
Beano, Topper, Dandy, Radio Fun.
The characters in each, I remember each one.
Only thing then on a child's mind each day
Was to wonder what game to play.
Nonstop running, shouting, always the odd fall.
Yes, I remember when I was small.

Daniel Godward was born in Limehouse, East London, to a working-class family. Life was tough, but it did enable him to develop a good sense of black humour. He enjoys reading and began writing poetry from an early age, inspired by the nonsense verse of Edward Lear and Lewis Carroll.

He has had a variety of jobs, starting early on in the racing profession and becoming the manager of a bookmaker. In the mid nineteen-seventies, he worked in accounts in the *Daily/Sunday Telegraph* newspaper. Although he loved the busy life of Fleet Street, in the late 'eighties, he took redundancy, managed a safe deposit company, then managed huge warehouses in Southeast London for a while before going back to the racing industry. He then turned a part-time acting job into a career, following his passion. He has had small roles in feature films and lead roles in small films. He has always written poetry in his spare time and now has a Facebook page (Danny Godward Poetry) devoted to his writing. He and his loving wife live in Kent, SE England, and they have three grown children all living abroad.

Printed in Great Britain
by Amazon